The Rockwool Foundation Research Unit

Unemployment and crime:
Experimental evidence of the causal
effects of intensified ALMPs on crime
rates among unemployed individuals

Signe Hald Andersen

University Press of Southern Denmark
Odense 2012

Unemployment and crime: Experimental evidence of the causal effects of intensified ALMPs on crime rates among unemployed individuals

Study Paper No. 38

Published by:
© The Rockwool Foundation Research Unit and
University Press of Southern Denmark

Copying from this book is permitted only within
institutions that have agreements with CopyDan,
and only in accordance with the limitations laid
down in the agreement

Address:
The Rockwool Foundation Research Unit
Sølvgade 10
DK-1307 Copenhagen K

Telephone   +45 33 34 48 00

Fax   +45 33 34 48 99

E-mail   forskningsenheden@rff.dk

Home page   www.rff.dk

ISBN 978-87-90199-64-7
ISSN 0908-3979
January 2012
Print run: 350
Printed by   Specialtrykkeriet Viborg A/S

Price: 60.00 DKK, including 25% VAT

Contents

Abstract 5

Introduction 6

Theory 7

    Crime and ALMPs 8

    Programs and gains from crime 9

    Programs and strain 9

    Programs and social control 10

    Programs and bad company 10

    Programs and the opportunity for crime 10

    Hypotheses 11

Data and method 12

    The experiment 12

    Data 13

    Method 14

    Variables 15

    Independent variable and controls 15

Results 16

    Selection problems? 20

Conclusion 22

References 23

Unemployment and crime: Experimental evidence of the causal effects of intensified ALMPs on crime rates among unemployed individuals

Signe Hald Andersen

Abstract
A number of studies investigate the extent to which levels of welfare benefits reduce crime among the unemployed. This paper expands this literature by testing whether the intensity of other welfare programs aimed at the unemployed affects their criminal activity, using evidence from a Danish social experiment that randomly assigned active labor market programs (ALMPs) of different levels of intensity to newly unemployed individuals. The results from a Negative Binomial model indicate that the intensity of ALMPs affects the number of crimes committed by the person during spells of unemployment.

Introduction

Unemployment and crime go hand in hand (Reilly & Witt, 1992; Britt, 1997; Elliott & Ellingworth, 1998; Kapuscinski et al., 1998; Witt et al., 1998; Lin, 2007; Buonanno & Montolio, 2008; Baron, 2008). The poverty risk induced by unemployment inclines unemployed individuals to seek alternative strategies for securing an income, including in some cases, criminal activities. And while poverty is a frequent consequence of becoming unemployed, unemployment also provides other motives for engaging in crime. Unemployment generates negative stimuli from social interactions, frees the individual from the social control imposed by institutions such as workplace and the moral judgment of colleagues, and promotes idlenss. These are all mechanisms that, according to theory, may affect criminal behavior during unemployment.

In most countries, however, the government takes various measures intended to reduce the negative consequences of unemployment. Such measures are highly likely to also affect crime among the unemployed by ameliorating the negative consequences of unemployment that may lead to criminal activity. One of the most obvious examples of such a measure is welfare benefits, which reduces the necessity for engaging in criminal activity as a method of maintaining an income (Zhang, 1997; Britt, 1997; Kapuscinski et al., 1998; Lin, 2007). In addition to providing welfare benefits, governments often also operate other programs that target the unemployed. Most Western countries require unemployed to make use of reemployment services that consist of elements such as mandatory meetings with caseworkers, courses on how to apply for jobs, compulsory participation in training courses etc. (for U.S. examples of such programs, see Plesca & Smith, 2007; Black et al., 2003; for European examples, see Kluve & Schmidt, 2002; Kluve, 2006). These active labor market programs (ALMPs), fulfill the dual purposes of helping the unemployed to find work and of monitoring their activities to ensure that they fulfill the requirements for receiving welfare benefit.

A number of studies analyze whether generous welfare benefits reduce crime among the unemployed. These studies show that benefit levels and crime levels are negatively correlated (e.g. at the state level), which indicates that economic deprivation is one important explanation for the link between unemployment and crime (Calvó-Armengol et al., 2007; Worrall, 2005; Farral, 2006; Savolainen, 2000; DeFronzo, 1997; Zhang, 1997; Devine et al. 1988; DeFronzo 1983, 1996). But while theory suggests that also ALMPs affect the link between unemployment and crime, we still have no evidence as to how these programs, and the intensity with which they are applied, affect crime among unemployed. Knowledge concerning this issue is important, as it will help to reveal the extent to which institutional measures taken during unemployment affect crime, and thereby clarify when unemployment leads to crime.

The present study addresses this shortcoming by analyzing whether crime levels among the unemployed vary with the intensity of the ALMPs to which they are exposed (i.e. I focus on crime committed during the unemployment spell). To investigate this question, the study exploits a social experiment in which newly unemployed individuals were randomly chosen to receive the standard package of ALMPs (the control group) or a package of similar, but intensified ALMPs, requiring higher levels of participation in job search and training courses, and exposing the unemployed to more social control (the treatment group). This type of design allows us to draw valid conclusions regarding the causal effect of intensified ALMPs on the criminal activity of unemployed persons.

Theory

According to general theories on crime, such as the crime/criminality theory of Hirschi and Gottfredson (Birkbeck & LaFree ,1993; Hirschi & Gottfredson, 1986; Clarke, 1980) and Wikström's situational action theory (Wikström, 2006, 2009) – the probability that a person commits a criminal act depends on two factors. First is his or her initial disposition to become involved in criminal activities and second is the specific situation in which the person engages, with whatever opportunities and motivations for crime that situation provides. According to the more specialized theories on crime and unemployment, being unemployed represents in itself a situation that increases both motivation and opportunity for crime:

In conventional economic theory, crime is a result of the rational actor's cost-benefit calculations in a given situation. This implies that a person's likelihood of committing crime increases when the value of the gains (e.g. the stolen goods or the excitement) from such activities relative to the cost (e.g. social stigma or possible imprisonment), exceeds the gains relative to the costs of legal activities (Becker, 1968). Here, unemployment increases criminal activity, because it reduces the cost of for example imprisonment (Becker, 1968; see also Lester, 1995; Thaler, 1997; Calvó-Armengol et al., 2007).

The sociological theories rely less on the rational actor and more on the importance of social institutions and interpersonal relationships. Here, strain theory argues that a person's likelihood of committing crime increases when he or she receives only negative stimuli from social interactions, i.e. when the person is not treated in the way he or she wishes to be treated and is unable to achieve desired goals, such as earning money, gaining labor status, etc. Unemployment therefore increases crime because it puts the individual in a situation where he or she is unable to achieve certain desired goals.

In addition, social control theory argues that a person's likelihood of committing a crime increases when no person or social institution monitors that person's actions, i.e. people are inclined towards deviant behavior when they no longer feel the pressure of society's norms. Unemployment thus increases criminal activity, because it frees the person from the conventional control applied by work place routines and association with colleagues. This makes him or her more likely to follow any inclination to engage in deviant activities.

Last, social learning theory argues that a person's likelihood of committing crime increases when he or she enters into positive relationships with deviant others, i.e. when the person gets into bad company (Agnew, 1992; Patacchini & Zenou, 2008). Since unemployment increases daily excessive time it also increases the probability that the person gets into bad company and starts engaging in criminal activities (Patacchini & Yves, 2007).

Crime and ALMPs
These theories on unemployment and crime do however also imply that ALMPs aimed at the unemployed affects their criminal activities.[1] This is due to the content and the working of these programs, which are roughly the same across all countries where they are applied.

Apart from welfare benefits and restrictions regarding entitlement to those benefits, ALMPs usually consist of two elements. First are the meetings between the unemployed person and his or her caseworker. These meetings have two purposes; they are intended both to help the unemployed person make plans for reentering the labor market, and to make sure that the person satisfies the requirements of the system (in Denmark, for example, an unemployed person must respond to a certain number of job advertisements per month in order to maintain his or her entitlement to benefits, and caseworkers check on this activity through the meetings). Second are the various types of job training programs; these are intended to upgrade the unemployed person's human capital, to facilitate contacts with potential employers, and to keep the unemployed person occupied. While both elements provide important help for the unemployed to find jobs, they also imply a significant element of social control. Importantly, the programs therefore also produce significant threat effects that have been found to make unemployed individuals more likely to find employment, i.e. to reduce the duration

---

[1] Note that there is no specific theory on the effect of ALMPs on crime, as the massive literature on the effects of these programs focuses on labor market outcomes such as earnings and reemployment opportunities (see Friedlander et al. (1997) for a review; see also Heckman et al., 1999; Greenberg et al., 2003; Fertig et al., 2006), and on the effect of participation on the well-being of the unemployed (Oddy et al., 1984; Korpi, 1997; Creed et al., 1998; Strandh, 2001; Machin & Creed, 2003; Andersen, 2008).

of the unemployment spell (see Friedlander et al, 1997 for a review; see also Heckman et al., 1999).

By these means, ALMPs thus restructure the unemployment experience, in that they require the unemployed to go to meetings with a caseworker, to apply for jobs, to participate in training programs, to take subsidized jobs, etc. This imposes a new structure on the everyday lives of the unemployed, and implies that they are involved in new types of situations. Since most of these programs also entail a significant threat effect, they tend to reduce the duration of the unemployment spells, thereby reducing the number of days and months that the individual is exposed to the potentially harmful effects of the unemployment. Thus, as crime depends on the opportunities and motivations existing in a given situation (see above), the various ways in which the ALMPs change the experience of unemployment, including the actual exposure to unemployment, could potentially affect the probability of an unemployed person committing crime.

The focus of this paper is on whether intensified versions of ALMPs, wherein the unemployed person meets with his or her caseworker more often, attends courses at an earlier stage in the unemployment spell, and is likely to exit unemployment at an earlier stage etc., have an effect on the amount of crime committed by the unemployed person (during the period of unemployment). This is the case first, if the theoretical perspectives presented above predict an effect of ALMPs on the criminal activities of the unemployed, and second, if the perspectives support the claim that an intensification of the programs also intensifies their effects.

Programs and gains from crime
According to Becker's theory, an unemployed person commits a crime if the expected gains from the crime exceed the expected costs. From this perspective, ALMPs affect criminal activity only during unemployment if participation also generates higher benefit levels or, more general, higher utility levels. Similarly, the intensity of programs also only matters if there is a correlation between intensity and benefit/utility levels.

Programs and strain
ALMPs could potentially reduce the strain experienced by the unemployed. According to Strandh (2001), the programs counteract some of the negative effects of unemployment, since job training programs provide new skills and enable unemployed individuals to engage in new and more specialized forms of labor market activity. ALMPs therefore increase an unemployed person's sense of mastery and hence his or her feeling of achieving desired goals, and this is likely to result in positive stimuli. While this implies that programs reduce the probability of an unemployed person committing a criminal act, it also implies that positive stimuli will increase with the increasing intensity of the program: If a sense of

mastery depends on learning new skills, and the intensified program facilitates more learning, then the higher level of intensity will produce more positive stimuli. This should then lead to a further reduction in crime.

On the other hand, however, some types of job training programs are notorious for being structured primarily in order to keep the unemployed occupied rather than to increase their human capital. In such cases the unemployed are likely to experience the programs as a waste of time, whereby the ALMPs probably do not create positive stimuli. The programs are then unlikely to reduce an unemployed person's probability of committing a criminal act. In fact, if an unemployed person feels that the program participation is really useless, it might even increase the negative stimuli experienced through unemployment and increase the probability of that person engaging in criminal activities. In this scenario, the negative stimuli will increase with the increasing level of intensity of the program.

Programs and social control
ALMPs expose the unemployed to more social control than pure unemployment without any ALMP. As explained above, they do this both through the meetings with caseworkers and through the job training schemes, which place the person involved in a social institution with rules and requirements (for example in an educational institution or a work place). If the social control explanation of the relationship between unemployment and crime is valid, we would expect ALMPs to reduce crime in comparison with the amount of crime that occurs in conditions of pure unemployment, and more intensive ALMPs to be even more efficient, as they imply increased social control.

Programs and bad company
According to the fourth explanation, unemployment increases a person's likelihood of committing a crime because additional leisure time available during unemployment spells increases the risk of the person getting into bad company. Since both the meetings with the caseworker and especially the job training programs reduce this idleness, also this explanation predicts that exposure to ALMPs decrease the likelihood of an unemployed person committing a crime. This effect is likely to increase with the intensity of the programs, because increased intensity reduces idleness even further.

Programs and the opportunity for crime
Last, ALMPs could potentially reduce the amount of crime committed by an unemployed person simply by shortening the period of time in which he or she is unemployed. According to general theories on crime, the number of crimes committed by an individual depends on the number of opportunities for crime that he or she experiences. Thus, if ALMPs make an individual more eager to find

work – a factor which is likely to shorten the duration of his or her unemployment – then the programs will reduce crime rates among the unemployed. As more intensive programs are likely to have stronger threat effects, thus further shortening spells of unemployment, intensified programs should reduce crime rates even further.

Hypotheses
Taken together, the theories do not produce a single clear-cut hypothesis on the link between ALMPs and crime. With Becker's theory the link between intensified programs and crime is conditioned on whether benefit or utility levels vary with this intensity, while part of the strain theory implies that intensified programs would increase the number of crimes committed by the unemployed. The remaining perspectives imply that intensified programs have increased negative effects (i.e. they reduce crime), but they disagree on why this is: The strain theory, the social control theory and the social learning theory claim that intensified programs reduce crime by changing the factors experienced during unemployment (i.e. the intensified positive stimuli and control, and the reduced interaction with delinquent peers). But while the general theories on crime accommodate these claims these theories also make separate contributions; intensified programs reduce crime by reducing the time period during which the individual is exposed to temptations to commit crime. Thus crime reduction comes about either through what the unemployed are exposed to, or by their being exposed to it for less time.

Because of these ambiguities, and because there are no previous findings to rely on, I suggest two contradictory hypotheses:

1. Intensified ALMPs lower the probability of an unemployed person committing a crime during a spell of unemployment either

    a. because the programs expose the unemployed to increased positive stimuli, increased utility and social control and because they reduce the likelihood of unemployed individuals getting into bad company, or

    b. because the increased threat effect of the intensified ALMPs shortens the duration of the unemployment spell

2. Intensified ALMPs raise the probability of an unemployed person committing a crime during the unemployment spell, because the mandatory aspects of the programs cause frustration, thereby exposing the unemployed person to negative stimuli.

Data and method

To analyze whether the intensity of ALMPs affects crime levels among the unemployed, I use Danish administrative data from a controlled social experiment that the Public Employment Service (PES) conducted in two Danish regions (Sønderjyllands County and Storstrøms County) from November 2005 to March 2006. The experimental setting allows us to assess the pure effect of the programs, and to make causal inference.

The experiment
In the experiment, all individuals who became newly unemployed[2] UI recipients[3] during the four months (n=5,184) were randomly selected for exposure to either standard ALMPs or intensified ALMPs. The date of birth determined the treatment assignment, as newly unemployed individuals who were born in the first half of a month (from the 1st to the 15th of a month) received the treatment, and newly unemployed individuals who were born in the second half of a month (from the 16th to the 31st of a month) acted as controls (Graversen & van Ours (2008) and Rosholm (2008) describe the experiment).

The aim of the experiment was to investigate whether intensified ALMPs affected the job search behavior of the unemployed. Hence, the control group received the standard package of ALMPs, which included meetings with caseworkers every third month and participation in activation programs after 12 months of unemployment. The law on active labor market policies also allowed the unemployed individuals to participate in a 6-week- long labor market program of their own choice during the first year of unemployment.

The treatment group faced far stricter measures, which differed from the standard measures in four ways. First, after 1.5 weeks of unemployment, the treatment group received a letter informing them that they were part of the experiment, and explaining the activities involved in the programs. Second, after 5 or 6 weeks, the treatment group members were obliged to participate in a job search program of 2 weeks duration, and after this program the treatment group had to attend meetings with their caseworker every week, or every second week. Third, the people in the treatment group had to participate in a training program of at least 3 months duration, before the end of the fourth month of unemployment. Fourth, if the

---

[2] A person is regarded as 'newly unemployed' when he or she has not been unemployed in the 12 months prior to the current unemployment spell.
[3] These are the insured unemployed, i.e. those who have insured themselves against unemployment prior to the event, and who therefore receive unemployment insurance benefits rather than welfare benefits during their unemployment. Unemployment insurance benefits are higher than welfare benefits

people in the treatment group had not found work within 6-7 months, their meetings with the caseworker were intensified still further, with the purpose of re-evaluating their job search strategy and of introducing new active measures (i.e. new activation programs).

While the experiment did not have any economic consequences for neither the treatment group nor the control group, it exposed the treatment group to far greater social control than the control group, and it significantly reduced the opportunities for idleness of the treatment group. The experiment also exposed individuals in the treatment group to the positive (and possible negative) stimuli and thus increased utility from program participation. In addition, previous studies show that the treated unemployed in the experiment responded to the increased threat of program participation by leaving unemployment at a faster rate than the controls (Graversen & van Ours, 2008; Rosholm, 2008), which means that the treated had fewer opportunities for crime than the controls. Overall, then, the experiment changed both the motivation and the opportunities for the treatment group to commit criminal acts during their period of unemployment compared the level of those factors for the control group.

Data

I use data from administrative registers. In Denmark all residents have a unique personal number which identifies them in a great many transactions, such as interactions with the welfare system, place of residence, work status and criminal behavior. Statistics Denmark conducts a yearly collection of the information registered with this personal number, and makes these data available in anonymous form for statistical and research purposes. This means that all Danish residents constitute a panel for which data are available as far back as 1980. In addition, I also have information from the PES which allows me to identify the unemployed individuals who participated in the social experiment.

The administrative data are highly suited for the purpose of this study, because they contain individual level data on criminal behavior. These data contain accurate records of the time and type of each criminal offence committed, and if and when a person was charged with and convicted of the offence. This means that I know whether a person committed a crime during the period of unemployment, which allows me to assess differences in the criminal behavior between the treatment group and the control group. This individual level information on criminal behavior is quite unique in an international context.

The social experiment involves 5,184 unemployed persons. I delete 31 observations for individuals who were assigned a treatment or control status erroneously (which I may check by comparing information on birth date from the registers with the information on treatment status), and observations for people (N=439) who leave unemployment before ever receiving unemployment benefits (which implies that they were assigned to a group but never entered the program). This leaves me with 4,714 observations, of which 2,329 receives the treatment and the rest, 2,385 are the controls.

Method

Since I have data from a social experiment I could in principle assess the effect of the intensified program on crime, simply by comparing the number of crimes committed by the treatment group during their unemployment spells with the number of crimes committed by the control group during their unemployment spells. The random assignment ensures that the two groups are similar in all aspects except for their treatment status, meaning that only the treatment status causes systematic differences in outcomes between the two groups. However, there are at least two arguments against this strategy.

First, as is evident from Table 1, the treated and the controls are not completely similar with regards to their background characteristics; there are significantly more immigrants and more 40- to 50-year-old individuals in the treatment group. Thus descriptive differences in the two group's crime rates during their period of unemployment could result from these differences in background characteristics, rather than from their different treatment statuses.

Second, hypothesis 1b concerns differences in the length of exposure to unemployment between the treated and the controls. Thus, to investigate this hypothesis we need to adjust for differences in length of exposure to unemployment to know whether any observed effect result from these differences.

Consequently, I choose an empirical strategy, where I first present the descriptive statistics for the differences in the crime rates for the two groups. Second, I present the results from a Negative Binomial regression model, where the only independent variable is participation status, third I present results from the same model where I adjust for exposure to unemployment and fourth, I present results from a Negative Binomial regression model which includes a range of controls, that adjust for the small observed differences in background characteristics between the treatment group and the control group. I use the Negative Binomial regression model, rather than a logistic regression or a linear model, because my dependent variable consists of the number of crimes committed by the individuals (as I describe below), and thus has the characteristics of a count variable. In addition, with the Negative Binomial model, I can easily take differences in each individual's exposure to unemployment into account (i.e., length of unemployment spells), and thus investigate hypothesis 1b. Finally, to test whether the results from the Negative Binomial model suffer from selection bias, caused by unobserved differences between the treatment and control groups, I conduct a robustness check using a difference-in-difference estimator. This estimator represents a state-of-the-art approach to causal inference, as it eliminates all observed and unobserved time in-variant differences, by comparing differences between treatment and control groups in changes in crime rates before and during unemployment

Variables
My dependent variable measures the number of convictions committed by each individual during the unemployment spell. This means, first that I do not, as is common in the literature distinguish between violent crime and property crime; the low crime rate compels me to merge these two together. Second, this dependent variable also includes convictions related to traffic offences. This is probably more unorthodox than merging categories of violent crime and property crime, as the reasons for traffic offences may diverge from reasons for other types of crime. For that reason, I also present the results from a model where the dependent variable does not contain traffic offences.

Table 1 shows the descriptive statistics for the two dependent variables. In both cases do individuals in the treatment group have lower average crime rates than the individuals in the control group. This difference is, however not significant for the dependent variable "all convictions except traffic offences". Thus during their period of unemployment, individuals in the treatment groups committed fewer crimes overall and there is a tendency that they also commit fewer crimes that are not related to traffic offences. The results section will describe these differences more thoroughly.

Independent variable and controls
My key independent variable is the individual's treatment status, and as mentioned earlier, 2,329 (49 percent) of the individuals in my sample receive the treatment – the intensified ALMPs – and 2,385 individuals act as controls.

Table 1 also shows the distribution of a range of standard control variables, such as previous convictions, gender, age and parenthood that I include in the model. As mentioned earlier, there are some systematic differences between the two groups. More people in the treatment group have an immigrant background and are between the ages of 40 and 50. Even though these differences are small, they are still non-negligible.

From Table 1 we also learn that, on average, the individuals in the control group have longer spells of unemployment than the individuals in the treatment group. This finding was expected, and it supports the findings of previous studies using data from the same experiment (see Graversen & van Ours, 2008). It demonstrates the fact that the treated are in fact less exposed to unemployment than the controls, as suggested earlier.

Table 1: Differences in means between the treatment group and the control group (standard deviation in parentheses)

	Treatment	Control	T-test for differences in means
All criminal convictions	0.018 (0.135)	0.029 (0.183)	2.14**
All criminal convictions, except traffic offences	0.004 (0.065)	0.008 (0.093)	1.55
Exposure variable: Duration of unemployment	4.235 (2.966)	4.967 (3.444)	7.81***
Controls			
No. of previous offences prior to unemployment (3 year period)	0.060 (0.322)	0.055 (0.346)	0.10
Convicted of at least one offence prior to unemployment (3 year period)	0.071	0.068	-0.51
Immigrant	0.071	0.054	-2.44**
Children	0.292	0.281	-0.61
Single	0.523	0.530	0.48
Age, <40 years old	0.486	0.498	0.77
Age, between 40 and 50 years old	0.260	0.236	1.89*
Level of education (1-7)	3.374 (1.303)	3.356 (1.315)	-0.45
Log (wages)	0.744 (8.248)	0.862 (8.106)	0.49
Female	0.417	0.422	0.34
No. of observations	2,329	2,385	

*** $p<0.01$; ** $p<0.05$; * $p<0.10$
Source: Own calculations based on data from Statistics Denmark

Results

Table 2 shows the first set of results, the purely descriptive ones, and as can be seen there is a tendency for the control group to receiving convictions more often than the treatment group.

Table 2: Descriptive results: Distribution of convictions (percentages in parentheses)

	All criminal convictions		All criminal convictions, except traffic offences	
No. of crimes/ convictions	Controls	Treated	Controls	Treated
0	2,324 (97.44)	2,286 (98.15)	2,367 (99.25)	2,319 (99.57)
1	54 (2.26)	43 (1.85)	17 (0.71)	10 (0.43)
2	7 (0.29)	0	1 (0.04)	0
3	0	0	0	0
4 or more	0	0	0	0

Source: Own calculations based on data from Statistics Denmark

Table 3 shows the results from the various Negative Binomial models. The first three rows show results from a model where I use all convictions as dependent variable, first in a simple model, without and with the adjustment for length of exposure to unemployment, and then in an expanded model where I include a number of controls. The last three rows show the same types of models, but with my other outcome variable, the one that measures all criminal convictions, except for traffic offences.

All the models produce significant and negative treatment effects. This demonstrates that being randomly selected into the treatment group and receiving intensified programs, lowers the probability of an unemployed individual being convicted of committing a crime – both traffic offences and other offences - during the unemployment. This then first of all allows me to reject hypothesis two: the intensified programs have an effect, and the effect does not increase the criminal actitivies of the treated. Second, but just as interesting, we observe that both models with and without adjustment for length of exposure to unemployment produce significant results. However, the effect of the intensified programs is less significant in models with the adjustment. This suggests that we cannot rule out either of hypotheses 1a and 1b, and that the total treatment effect includes both different lengths of exposure to unemployment for the treatment and the control groups, and the two group's different experiences during unemployment.

Unfortunately my data do not allow me to test the different explanations that constitute hypothesis 1a: The administrative data do not contain information concerning the amount of leisure time during unemployment, increased sense of mastery due to program participation or increased social control caused by both program participation and meetings with the caseworker. However we do know from the registers the extent of participation in training programs among the unemployed (i.e. one of the elements of the programs). The registers show that average length of participation among the treated is 1.1 months, while it was 0.4 months for the controls (the difference is statistically significant). Controlling for participation in the models provides an initial unraveling of the program effect: It separates out the effect of belonging to either of the two groups, treatment or control, which involves a range of differences, and the effect of one of these differences, i.e. the increased participation in training programs, on the treated. However, as explained in the theory section, training releases each of the three mechanisms of the treatment effect – it reduces time for idleness, increases the sense of mastery and increases the social control. Thus, the estimated effect of participation in training programs does not provide us with much additional knowledge on the theoretical mechanisms causing the treatment effect. Only more subjective data on the unemployment experience will provide such knowledge.[4]

---

[4] Note that a control for program participation does not alter any of the conclusions of this paper.

Results

Table 3: The models, simple and expanded, with and without exposure

Dep. variable	Model 1a: All criminal convictions	Model 1b: All criminal convictions	Model 1c: All criminal convictions	Model 2a: All criminal convictions. except traffic offences	Model 2b: All criminal convictions. except traffic offences	Model 2c: All criminal convictions. except traffic offences
Participant	-0.43 (0.13)***	-0.28 (0.12)**	-0.45 (0.13)***	-0.62 (0.28)**	-0.54 (0.30)*	-0.55 (0.27)**
Age<40			0.42 (0.37)			-0.03 (0.63)
40=<age<50			0.35 (0.60)			-0.91 (0.93)
Children. age 0-6			-0.08 (0.17)			-0.51 (0.40)
Number of crimes committed past 3 years			0.04 (0.06)*			-0.13 (0.19)
Convicted of at least one offence in past 3 years			0.87 (0.28)***			1.60 (0.63)**
Immigrant			0.16 (0.35)			-0.89 (0.98)
Single			0.80 (0.27)***			-0.01 (0.72)
Level of education			-0.13 (0.07)**			-0.46 (0.21)**
Tenure			-0.27 (0.44)			-1.22 (0.60)**
Log(wages)			0.00 (0.01)			0.46 (0.41)
Female			-0.70 (0.22)***			-1.22 (0.60)**
Intercept	-3.56 (0.12)***	-5.15 (0.13)***	-3.06 (0.67)***	-4.83 (0.18)***	-6.40 (0.19)***	-2.74 (2.33)
Exposure	No	Yes	No	No	Yes	No
Alpha	4.51 (2.41)	3.60 (2.11)	1.89 (1.33)	9.77 (9.84)	22.88 (6.89)	-1.27 (2.50)
Wald χ2	10.72***	5.12**	236.28***	4.75**	3.26*	7539.00***

*** $p<0.01$; ** $p<0.05$; * $p<0.10$
Note: The models take into account that the unemployed individuals are clustered in municipalities
Source: Own calculations based on data from Statistics Denmark

In addition to the treatment effects, models 1c and 2c also show that previous crime matter for crime committed during unemployment, and that level of education and tenure at the labor market is important. We also see that the female unemployed commit less crime than the male unemployed.

However, as one cannot compare raw coefficients across Negative Binomial models, Table 4 shows two versions of the marginal effects, evaluated at the averages of the sample values and at the sample mean of the regressors. These results clearly indicate that the program effect depends on the model specification. In models 1a and 2a – the simpler model where I do not take unemployment exposure into account – the intensified program reduces crime by 0.01 respectively 0.003 conviction per person. The effect is approximately one third lower when I take exposure into account in the first model (1a). This indicates that differences in the length of the exposure to unemployment, is an important part of the treatment effect.

The effects are admittedly rather small, as they suggest that the program prevents the entire treatment group from committing approximately 24 respectively 8 crimes during their unemployment spell (2,329 treated individuals * 0.01 ≈ 24, or * 0.0033 ≈ 8). However it is important to consider the personal, societal and economic costs of each of these crimes; consider the personal and economic costs of the crime for the victim, the social cost of having a more crime ridden society, where people feel the need to protect themselves and their families, and the economic costs of processing cases of criminal activities. From that perspective the crime-reducing effects of a labor market program that is already being implemented for other reasons is a useful added bonus.

Table 4: Marginal effects of intensified ALMPs on crime committed during unemployment

Dep. variable	Model 1a: All convictions	Model 1b: All convictions	Model 1c: All convictions	Model 2a: All convictions. except traffic offences	Model 2b: All convictions. except traffic offences	Model 2c: All convictions. except traffic offences
Average marginal effects	-0.0102 (0.0034)***	-0.0066 (0.0030)**	-0.0097 (0.0039)***	-0.0038 (0.0019)**	-0.0036 (0.0022)*	-0.0034 (0.0017)*
Marginal effect at the mean	-0.0100 (0.0032)***	-0.0064 (0.0029)**	-0.0070 (0.0029)***	-0.0036 (0.0017)**	-0.0034 (0.0019)*	-0.0011 (0.0011)

*** $p<0.01$; ** $p<0.05$; * $p<0.10$
Source: Own calculations based on data from Statistics Denmark

Selection problems?

As illustrated in Table 1, the two samples differ in terms of some of the background characteristics of the participants. While I control for these differences in the Negative Binomial models, the two samples could differ with respect to unobserved characteristics, despite the random treatment assignment. If that is the case, my results may suffer from important biases that invalidate my conclusions. To investigate this possibility, I conduct further analysis using a difference-in-difference estimator. This estimator represents a state-of-the-art approach to causal inference, as it removes all observed and unobserved time-in-variant differences by comparing differences between treatment and control groups in changes in crime rates before and during unemployment. Equation 1 explains the procedure. Here, Y_0 is the pre-treatment crime and Y_1 is crime during unemployment, T respectively C signifies treatment status (T are the treated and C are the controls).

[1] $\quad \hat{d}_D = (\bar{Y}_1^T - \bar{Y}_0^T) - (\bar{Y}_1^C - \bar{Y}_0^C)$

Following equation 1, the difference-in-difference parameter, $\hat{d}_D$, is then calculated as the differences between the two groups (T and C) in the change in crime levels before and during unemployment $(\bar{Y}_1 - \bar{Y}_0)$.

Table 5 shows the results from the difference-in-difference estimation. I show calculations for the two different outcome measures, all criminal convictions and all criminal convictions except traffic, and results that account for duration of exposure to unemployment (I account for exposure by dividing total number of crime with duration of unemployment). I measure pre-unemployment crime as the average monthly crime rate in the 36 months that precedes the unemployment spell, and crime during unemployment as total crime (except for when I account for exposure to unemployment).

From Table 5 we learn that the treated unemployed commit less crime during unemployment than the controls. The effect is significant when I use all convictions without accounting for exposure and all convictions except traffic offenses, with exposure. Importantly, the effect is almost significant at a 10 per cent level, in the model with all convictions except traffic as outcome, where I do not account for exposure. Thus according to the difference-in-difference model, the program effect on all convictions (including traffic offences) boils down to an effect of the length of the exposure to unemployment, and is, apparently unrelated to the intensified content. In contrast the results from the difference-in-difference estimator show that it is mainly this content that drives the program effect on the outcome "all convictions, except traffic offences". This last finding is quite surprising as it shows the opposite of what we found in the Negative Binomial models. Thus it seems that to some extent does selection problems drive the results for the outcome "all convictions except traffic" and that the true program effect primarily consists in the content of the intensified program, rather than the shortened exposure to unemployment experienced by the treated unemployed. Overall, it seems that the intensity of the ALMPs still matter for both my outcomes, when controlling for possible sources of selection.

Table 5: Results derived from difference-in-difference estimator

	Average monthly crime rate before unemployment	No. of crimes committed during unemployment	Differences in crime rates before and during unemployment
All convictions			
Controls	0.0017	0.0285	0.0270
Treated	0.0017	0.0185	0.0168
t-test for differences in means	-0.14	2.14**	2.16**
All convictions, accounting for exposure			
Controls	0.0017	0.0067	0.0050
Treated	0.0017	0.0046	0.0029
t-test for differences in means	-0.14	1.47	1.50
All convictions except traffic			
Controls	0.0015	0.0080	0.0064
Treated	0.0017	0.0043	0.0026
t-test for differences in means	-0.0001	1.56	1.62
All convictions except traffic, accounting for exposure			
Controls	0.0015	0.0025	0.0010
Treated	0.0017	0.0012	-0.0005
t-test for differences in means	-0.0001	1.56	1.65*

*** $p<0.01$; ** $p<0.05$; * $p<0.10$
Source: Own calculations based on data from Statistics Denmark

Conclusion

The aim of this paper was to test whether intensified ALMPs affect the number of crimes committed during unemployment. Evidence from a Danish social experiment indicates that the intensity of the ALMP does affect the number of crimes committed by an unemployed person. Thus, whereas these programs might not have any employment effects (as found in numerous previous studies), they seem to have other important implications for the participants, and in consequence, for society.

While this study focuses on the intensity of ALMPs – that is, more or less time spent participating in the program – one may also claim that it provides information on the effect of program participation vs. no program participation: To the extent that intensified programs reduce crime among the unemployed, the mere participation in a program should also have an effect. Thus, seen from the perspective of politicians and administrators who wish to reduce crime, exposing the unemployed to ALMPs of any intensity, will have that effect.

As mentioned in the introduction, this is the first study to analyze how the intensity of ALMPs affects the link between unemployment and crime, and much more work is needed to understand the full implications of these programs. One important step would be to identify exactly how the programs work to reduce crime. Is it the increased social control or the reduced strain which matters most, or is the reduced time for idleness a better explanation? This type of analysis will not only facilitate the discovery of interesting information about the explanatory powers of the various theories concerning unemployment and crime, but it will also provide an important tool for drawing policy implications from the analyses. Unfortunately, the nature of my data does not allow me to conduct such an analysis in this study.

References

Agnew, Robert (1992): Foundation for a General Strain Theory of Crime and Delinquency. *Criminology*, 30(1): 47-87.

Andersen, Signe Hald (2008): The Short- and Long-Term Effects of Government training on Subjective Well-being. *European Sociological Review*, 24(4): 451-462.

Baron, Stephen W. (2008): Street Youth Unemployment, and Crime: Is It That Simple? Using General Strain Theory to Untangle the Relationship. *Canadian Journal of Criminology and Criminal Justice*, July, 2008: 399-434.

Becker, Gary S. (1968): Crime and Punishment: An Economic Approach. *Journal of Political Economy*, 76 (2): 169-217.

Birkbeck, Christopher & LaFree, Gary (1993): The Situational Analysis of Crime and Deviance. *Annual Review of Sociology*, 19: 113-137.

Black, Dan A., Smith, Jeffrey A., Berger, Mark C., & Noel, Brett J. (2003): Is the Threat of reemployment Services more Effective Than the Services Themselves? Evidence from Random Assignment in the UI System. *The American Economic Review*, 93(4): 1313-1327.

Britt, Chester L. (1997): Reconsidering the Unemployment and Crime Relationship: Variation by Age Group and Historical Period. *Journal of Quantitative Criminology*, 13(4): 405-428.

Buonanno, Paolo & Montolio, Daniel (2008): Identifying the socio-economic and demographic determinants of crime across Spanish provinces. *International Review of Law and Economics*, 28: 89-97.

Calvó-Armengol, Antoni, Verdier, Thierry & Zenou, Yves (2007): Strong and weak ties in employment and crime. *Journal of Public Economics*, 91: 203-233.

Clarke, R. V. G. (1980): "Situational" Crime Prevention: Theory and Practice. *British Journal of Criminology*, 20(2): 136-147.

Creed, P. A., Bloxsome, T. D. & Johnston, K. (2001). Self-esteem and self-efficacy outcomes for unemployed individuals attending occupational skills training programs. *Community, Work & Family*, 4(3), 286-303.

DeFronzo, James (1983): Economic Assistance to Impoverished Americans – Relationship to Incidence of Crime. *Criminology*, 21 (119): 119-136.

DeFronzo, James (1996): Welfare and Burglary. *Crime and Delinquency*, 42(2): 223-230.

DeFronzo, James (1997): Welfare and Homicide. *Journal of Research in Crime and Delinquency*, 34(3): 395-406.

Devine, Joel A., Sheley, Joseph F., & Smith, M. Dwayne (1988): Macroeconomic and Social-Control Policy Influences on Crime Rate Changes, 1948-1985. *American Sociological Review*, 53(3): 407-420.

Elliott, Caroline & Ellingworth, Dan (1998): Exploring the relationship between unemployment and property crime. *Applied Economic Letters*, 5: 527-530.

Farrall, Stephen (2006): 'Rolling back the state': Mrs. Thatcher's criminological legacy. *International Journal of the Sociology of Law*, 34: 256-277.

Fertig, M., Schmidt, C. M. & Schneider, H. (2006). Active labor market policy in Germany – Is there a successful policy strategy? *Regional Science and Urban Economics*, 36(1), 399-400.

Friedlander, D., Greenberg, D. H. & Robins, P. K. (1997). Evaluating Government Training Programs for the Economically Disadvantaged. *Journal of Economic Literature*, 35(4), 1809-1855.

Graversen, Brian Krogh & Jan C. van Ours (2008). How to help unemployed find jobs quickly; Experimental evidence from a mandatory activation program. *Journal of Public Economics*, 92, 2020-2035.

Greenberg, D. H., Michalopoulos, C. & Robins, P. K. (2003). A Meta-Analysis of Government –Sponsored training Programs. *Industrial and Labor Relations Review*, 57(1), 31-53.

Heckman, J. J., Lalonde, R. & Smith, J. (1999). The Economics and Econometrics of Active Labour Market Programs. *Handbook of Labor Economics*, 3.

Hirschi, T. & Gottfredson, M. (1986). The distinction between crime and criminality. In Hartnage, T. F. & Silverman, R. A. (ed.). *Critique and explanation: Essays in honor of Gwynne Nettler*. New Brunswick, NJ: Transaction: 55-69

Kapuscinski, Cezary A., Braithwaite, John & Chapman, Bruce (1998): Unemployment and Crime: Toward Resolving the Paradox. *Journal of*

Quantitative Criminology, 14(3): 215-243.

Kluve, Jochen & Schmidt, Christoph M. (2002): Active policy evaluation. Problems, methods and results. *Economic Policy*, 17(35): 409-448.

Kluve, Jochen (2006): The Effectiveness of European Active Labor Market Policy. *IZA Discussion Paper*, 2018.

Korpi, T. (1997). Is utility related to employment status? Employment, unemployment, labor market policies and subjective well being among Swedish youth. *Labour Economics*, 4, 125-147.

Lester, Bijou Yang (1995): Property crime and unemployment: a new perspective. *Applied Economic Letters*, 2: 159-162.

Lin, Ming-Jen (2007): Does Unemployment Increase Crime. *The Journal of Human resources*, 43(2): 413-436.

Machin, M. A. & Creed, P. A. (2003). Understanding the Differential Benefits of Training for the Unemployed. *Australian Journal of Psychology*, 55(2), 104-113.

Oddy, M., Donovan, A. & Pardoe, R. (1984). Do government training schemes for unemployed school leavers achieve their objectives? A psychological perspective. *Journal of Adolescence*, 7: 377-385.

Patacchini, Eleonora & Zenou, Yves (2008): The strength of weak ties in crime. *European Economic Review*, 52: 209-236.

Plesca, Miana and Jeffrey Smith (2007): Evaluating Multi-Treatment Programs: Theory and Evidence from the U.S. Job Training Partnership Act. *Empirical Economics*, 32(2-3): 491-528.

Reilly, Barry & Witt, Robert (1992): Crime and Unemploymet in Scotland: An Econometric Analysis using regional Data. *Scottish Journal of Political Economy*, 39(2): 213-228.

Rosholm, Michael (2008): Experimental Evidence on the Nature of the Danish Employment Miracle. *IZA Discussion Paper*, 3620.

Savolainen, Jukka (2000): Inequality, Welfare State, and Homicide: Further Support for the Institutional Anomie Theory. *Criminology*, 38(4): 1021-1042.

Strandh, M. (2001). State Program and Mental Well being Among the

Unemployed. *Journal of Social Policy*, 30(1): 57-80.

Thaler, Richard (1977): An Econometric Analysis of Property Crime. Interaction between Police and Criminals. *Journal of Public Economics*, 8: 37-51.

Wikström, Per-Olav H. (2006): Individuals, settings, and acts of crime: situational mechanisms and the explanation of crime. In Per-Olav H. Wikström and Robert Sampson (eds.): *The Explanation of Crime: Context, mechanisms and development*. 61-107. Cambridge: Cambridge University Press.

Wikström, Per-Olav H. (2009): Crime propensity, criminogenic exposure and crime involvement in early to mid adolescence. *Monatsschrift für Kriminologie und Strafrechtsreform*, 92, 253-266.

Witt, Robert, Clarke, Alan & Fielding, Nigel (1998): Crime, earnings inequality and unemployment in England and Wales. *Applied Economic Letters*, 5: 265-267.

Worrall, John L. (2005): Reconsidering the relationship Between Welfare Spending and Serious Crime: A panel Data Analysis with Implications for Social Support Theory. *Justice Quarterly*, 22(3): 364-391.

Zhang, Junsen (1997): The Effect of Welfare Programs on Criminal Behaviour: A Theoretical and Empirical Analysis. *Economic Inquiry*, XXXV: 120-137.